LEADERSHIP 101

o·······●

101 observations in 101 words
to inspire those who find themselves in charge.

TONY HARRIS

Published by Clink Street Publishing 2022

Copyright © 2022

First edition.

ISBN: 978-1-914498-80-0 – paperback
978-1-914498-81-7 – ebook

If your actions inspire others
to dream more, learn more,
do more and become more,
you are a leader.

"

JOHN QUINCY ADAMS

Diagnosed Depressive ○········● 6th US President

INTRODUCTION

They say that "some are born great, some achieve greatness, some have greatness thrust upon them". Most leaders will recognize that final reference, as they embark on their new odyssey of huge responsibility, often, with very little guidance.

Many "great" figures have achieved "great" things in similar circumstances. They were also marked out for their talents and attributes, even though they too, probably considered themselves unlikely leadership material.

You're not the first, you won't be the last, but you're about to surprise yourself. You'll be amazed how much of a leader you already are.

Good luck – not that you'll need it.

> Sustaining an audience
>
> is hard. It demands a
>
> consistency of thought,
>
> of purpose and of action
>
> over a long period of time. "

BRUCE SPRINGSTEEN

High school loner ○·······● The Boss

ON
HOW TO
SHOW UP

The elevation to leadership can appear daunting, requiring, as it does, certain necessary changes. However, it is important to understand what kind of leader you are.

Are you hands-on? Are you demonstrative?

Do you communicate regularly or only in special circumstances?

These constitute only a fraction.

Think hard about your operating style because you need to retain the characteristics that brought you to this point. Don't become someone you're not.

Your team needs consistency and consequently the ability to adapt without fuss to your methods. If you're erratic they cannot settle nor find a suitable working rhythm that brings results effortlessly.

Self-confidence
is the first requisite of
great undertakings.

"

SAMUEL JOHNSON

Lived with Tourette Syndrome ○·······● Created the first definitive Dictionary
of the English Language

ON
RETURNING
THE FAITH

Because those around you have faith in your ability, you will have earned your leadership position. It is their trust that has put you where you now find yourself.

Of course, modesty forces you to question how this has been achieved – only an arrogant leader could think they were guaranteed elevation. You are allowed to remind yourself that you are genuinely there on merit.

Not believing in yourself will be distracting and will hamper your own efforts and those of your team. Their trust deserves your robust and sure-footed leadership.

Reward their confidence in you by reflecting the same in yourself.

If we wait for the moment when
everything, absolutely everything
is ready, we shall never begin.

"

IVAN TURGENEV

Civil service clerk ○‥‥‥‥● Major Russian fiction writer

ON GETTING STARTED

The leader of any enterprise always strives to create a perfect result, where every element and component has been stress-tested until it works in perfect synchronization.

Your output is the objective.

Input is different.

The temptation to delay while waiting for all elements to be in place is understandable. However, to get your project underway is more important. There will undoubtedly be adjustments, alterations, and outside factors previously unconsidered, and time can become your biggest enemy. Your schedule always needs flexibility, so kick off when enough – not all – is in place.

Because it's not how you start, it's how you finish.

A leader who
arrives in a new setting,
or inherits a big role,

needs to curb the
impulse to display
his manhood.

"

SIR ALEX FERGUSON

Sacked by St Mirren ○·······● Won more trophies than any other manager in
football history

ON
DAY ONE

They say you never get the chance to make another first impression but that is not entirely true for new leaders. The mistake is to think that you must assert your authority immediately, whereas you should actually be prepared to build an air of mystery around yourself initially.

Leadership requires perspective, so allow your new environment to adapt to you, while you adapt to it. Let your team sample your abilities gradually – not with a bombastic opening salvo.

Your informed decision-making will give them enough opportunity to form an impression of your operating style that is accurate and more considered.

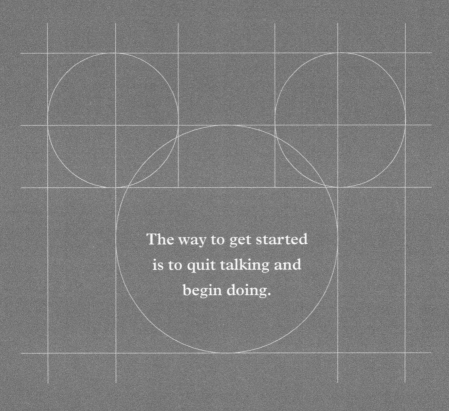

The way to get started
is to quit talking and
begin doing.

,,

WALT DISNEY

Paper boy ○·······● Pioneer of film animation

ON
SYMBOLS
OF CHANGE

When embarking on a new leadership position there is no better way of demonstrating that you mean business than making a positive change quickly – however small.

It may be a process, a routine or even something as trivial as seating arrangements, so take your team's counsel. If you can quickly gauge something simple that could be corrected without any undue stress, then make it happen. This change will inevitably make your team feel you listen, you collaborate, and you're geared to making things happen.

Even the smallest alteration to the previous dynamic can clearly signify there's a new sheriff in town.

Don't accept the old order.
Get rid of it.

"

JOHN LYDON

Suffered spinal meningitis ◦┈┈┈● Punk pioneer

ON BREAKING WITH THE PAST

People do not always accept change; either through fear of the unknown or a lack of appetite for learning something new. Often this is buried under shrill claims of tradition and history.

Your duty is to improve operations. So don't be hidebound by what you are told has worked in the past, but clearly is far less effective now. It requires sensitivity naturally to break long-cherished methodologies but improvements cannot be achieved without the courage to embrace them. Frame your moves as an evolution rather than a revolution.

For those, who stubbornly refuse to change, however, there can be no place.

The eye of the master will do more work than both of his hands.

"

BENJAMIN FRANKLIN

Apprentice printer at 12 ○·······● Founding Father of the United States

ON
THE BIGGER
PICTURE

Leadership is often equated with "seeing the bigger picture" or "helicoptering" because your viewpoint allows you crucially to analyse an undertaking in its entirety and from many angles. Furthermore, it presents the opportunity to highlight details that those closer to the process, may miss – details which could adversely affect the outcome.

Initially, this might meet with your team's frustration, but not passing on your analysis will undermine the value of their work.

This vantage point makes you the sole representative legitimately positioned to give a project the comprehensive scrutiny required, followed by constructive feedback.

You are duty-bound always to use it.

Let your **yeah** be **yeah**. "

JIMMY CLIFF

Worked on a vegetable truck o······• First internationally acclaimed Reggae artist

ON STRAIGHT TALKING

A key characteristic that can mark out great leaders is clarity; clarity of purpose, clarity of decision-making and particularly clarity of communication.

Unclear words lead to unclear actions and from there, confusion. Teams need to gain a sense of your decisiveness, if you seek their trust and respect. They must believe that every facet is operating to the same instruction.

Situations are always fluid so a decision may have to be superseded. Irrespective of that, as long as the communication is clear then any disruption can always be minimized.

Leadership always requires flexibility, but this must never cross over into ambiguity.

Even a genius asks questions.

TUPAC SHAKUR

Childhood spent living in shelters ○·······● Sold over 75 million records worldwide

ON
NOT KNOWING

Leadership will involve you in discussions over all areas of the enterprise – of some, you may have only had a cursory experience previously. The temptation can be to feign knowledge for fear of appearing ignorant.

Why should you know already about matters which do not fall naturally into your area of expertise? Particularly bespoke processes, technical aspects or (most annoyingly) jargon.

It is more dangerous to continue blithely without being clear. You have to have the maximum information possible to make considered decisions. Teams respect honesty and humility, by showing your desire to discover more.

So always be sure to ask.

> If you can't explain something simply,
> you don't understand it well.

ALBERT EINSTEIN

Passed over for promotion in Swiss Patent Office   ○·······●   Developed the Theory
for not mastering machine technology   of Relativity

ON
JARGON

Leaders sit at the centre of communications, so they need clear briefings. However, often the information they receive is highly technical, and these specialist reports use jargon that enhances their own sense of intelligence (sometimes very deliberately) but obscures clear comprehension

You are not expected to be skilled in every field of expertise, so insisting on clarity in layman's terms, can never be interpreted as a sign of intellectual weakness.

Make sure experts break down the details, so your conclusions can be passed on with equal simplicity and without misinterpretation. After all, you will always be accountable for the ultimate outcome.

Leaders
must invoke
an alchemy of
great vision.

"

HENRY KISSINGER

Refugee from Nazi Germany ○·······● US Secretary of State

ON
SHARING
THE VISION

A position of leadership can leave you feeling incredibly isolated. People will treat you differently, often with a sense of guarded caution; perhaps they'll think twice about approaching you directly.

Because you make the key decisions, nobody wants to portray themselves negatively in front of you. What might have once been an easy-going relationship can seem distant.

But now you have the vantage point to plot out a mission in its entirety. It's only lonely while you wait to bring others up there with you, to see that mission and the ensuing benefits for themselves.

So, share that view whenever possible.

I must govern the clock,
not be governed by it.

GOLDA MEIR

Refugee from Russian Empire ○·······• Prime Minister of Israel

ON
TIME KEEPING

With so many demands upon them, new leaders soon realise that their most precious commodity is time. It must be guarded assiduously.

Not keeping to schedule seems to be a transgression that is relatively forgivable. However, if time is so precious then, schedules should be treated as sacred. For leaders, this is constantly important because it sets a standard for promptness that you expect others to follow. Reporting should be clear and action points equally so – and all kept within the allotted timeframe.

Make it clear that your time is not elastic, and nobody should ever attempt to make it so.

Dressing well
is a kind of
good manners.

"

TOM FORD

NYU Dropout ○········● Successful fashion designer and film maker

ON LOOKING THE PART

Being in a leadership position will mean all eyes will naturally swivel towards you, making you the centre of attention. However, your appearance should never be a cause of conversation. If so, it detracts from the message you want to convey.

So whether it's a uniform, or sports kit or even dress-down Friday, take pride in your appearance. It shows respect for your position, your mission and the people with whom you operate.

By all means, dress for what suits you but make sure it is always appropriate to the circumstances. Your direction will be on point, if you are too.

Electric communication will never be a substitute for the face of someone who with their soul encourages another person to be brave and true.

"

CHARLES DICKENS

Boot-blacking warehouse labourer ○·······● Greatest novelist of the Victorian age

ON
FACE TO FACE

In a world of email and text, it is very easy to forget the value of meeting someone face to face. Whilst there is no doubting the speed and convenience modern communications provide, important business is always best conducted in person whenever possible.

Explanation is regularly required which, more often than not, requires dialogue. Your intention, encouragement and subsequent enthusiasm will be far more credible when they are backed up by your presence rather than as words on a screen.

The action of taking time and showing a personal interest in individuals is always appreciated and so creates a lasting impression.

Showing off is the fool's idea of glory.

BRUCE LEE

Restaurant dishwasher ○·······● Martial arts pop culture icon

ON SHOWBOATING

Leaders should never feel the need to grandstand. Some mistakenly decide that constantly demonstrating their knowledge to the team will symbolize why they are in charge, but it is more likely to be seen as arrogance or vanity, damaging the respect towards their authority.

Instead, let others show you what they know and correspondingly use your knowledge as evidence to support or counter them in the decision-making process. You may well believe you know more about a subject, but only exhibit this if situations absolutely demand.

Intelligence is not just a breadth of knowledge but the discernment to use it carefully.

The world belongs
to the articulate.

EDWIN H. LAND

Never completed his studies ○········● Co-founder of the Polaroid Corporation

ON DIRECTING NOT ORDERING

Though leadership requires a constant round of decision-making, that pressure should never lead to the barking of orders. It implies a loss of control and will create an atmosphere of confused resentment.

It can admittedly feel strange asking others to carry out your instructions, but don't forget that implementation is essentially their role. They will however genuinely appreciate your communication if it clearly explains the background to the task and why they have been chosen to do it.

Ultimately, it acknowledges their underlying desire to understand what potential benefit there is for them, either individually or as part of the team.

Ag

If speaking is silver,

Au

then listening is gold.

"

TURKISH PROVERB

ON
JUST
LISTENING

Those who assume leadership positions often make the mistake of believing that they need to pronounce on everything immediately. It is well-intentioned because it shows a forthright determination to control situations. However, snap judgements can often rebound very badly.

The true skill is in the capacity to listen first.

It seems obvious but often others already have the answer – sometimes unwittingly – and getting a handle on all the facts will inevitably lead to a more satisfactory result. It crucially allows the whole team to feel ownership of the problem and subsequent solution.

Remember – nobody ever listened themselves out of a job.

You've
got to be on
the ball from the
minute you step out
into that spotlight. You
gotta know exactly what
you're doing every second
on that stage, otherwise the
act goes right into the bathroom.

"

FRANK SINATRA

Damaged eardrum at birth   ○·······●   "The greatest singer of the 20ᵗʰ century"

ON CULTIVATING IMAGE

Good leaders do not seek out personal celebrity but paradoxically they still need to be particularly image-conscious regardless of being a big personality or a quiet operator.

Eyes are upon you constantly and so you need to manage the impression you put out. Follow the standards you expect from others. Retain a consistent level of proactive positivity. Radiate the projected success of your team and their mission. People want and need to believe in you.

Popularity, though a welcome side-effect, is not the goal – but enduring and universal respect should be. Credibility is the essence of any leader's star quality.

> You don't need a weatherman to know which way the wind blows.
>
> "

BOB DYLAN

College drop-out ∘·········• Multiple Grammy, Pulitzer Prize, Golden Globe & Academy Award winner and №bel Laureate.

ON
GUT INSTINCTS

Leaders are inevitably marked out for their role because of their previous series of good, instinctive decisions. However, when taking up the mantle, an overwhelming information deluge will follow, then a truckload of opinions, and finally a sudden urgency to assign next actions.

Understandably, you may feel the need to weigh up every aspect with extra caution and attention because responding instinctively seems irresponsible when you are comparatively new to the position.

Don't silence your instinct because you are faced with so much new evidence. Remember it has taken you to the right places before; trust what it tells you now.

They don't care how
much you know

until they
know how much
you care.

"

THEODORE ROOSEVELT

Chronic asthmatic o·······• Leader of the "Rough Riders" volunteer cavalry &
26th US President

ON COLLECTIVE CULTURE

As leader, you are the custodian of the collective culture. This may have been developed over many generations or you may be trying to establish it within a new team. The similarity is that both groups can be more tightly bound together by marks, rituals or traditions.

As long as they follow responsible and inclusive behaviour, you should look to support group initiatives wherever possible. They establish esprit de corps and naturally integrate new members into the group quickly.

These behaviours will signify your group as special and, consequently, happy to transmit their unwavering loyalty whilst pushing themselves to peak performance.

You have a meeting to make a decision, not to decide on the question.

"

BILL GATES

Bullied as a kid ○·······● Co-founder of Microsoft

ON
THE VALUE OF
MEETINGS

Everybody feels the need to take time out of their leader's hectic schedule with a flood of meetings. But as meetings cannot be avoided, look to get the most from them.

Most importantly, keep to the schedule and show enthusiasm – the subject is probably of paramount concern to the invited audience.

Enter all meetings with these intentions: firstly, exhibiting imagination, then tightening the bonds between your team, and finally making clear and actionable decisions. If a meeting is unlikely to exhibit these, then you should reconsider the value of your attendance.

Meetings should be considered a showcase for your leadership strength.

Nobody can do everything well, so learn how to delegate responsibility to other winners and then hold them accountable for their decisions.

"

GEORGE FOREMAN

Incarcerated as a teenager ○········● Olympic Gold Medallist, World Heavyweight Boxing Champion, entrepreneur & preacher

ON
THE ART OF
DELEGATION

As a leader, you may have ultimate responsibility, but you cannot carry out every single task yourself. There are always areas where others have more expertise so delegate to them and let them get on with their task. You must not become a bottleneck.

This will sometimes entail giving up authority over an area to others better equipped. However, always build a process that allows for regular updates.

In understanding delegation, you maximise your ability to think strategically and imaginatively about the overall objectives.

Your role is to identify the problems and put together the best structure to deal with them.

He who does not know
how to look back at where he came
from will never get to his destination.

"

JOSE RIZAL

A frail child o·······• Philippine national hero

ON
STICKING
TO THE BRIEF

Whilst leaders are always focused on momentum and progress, it is important that they always make time to look back at the original brief for their enterprise.

Sometimes it is all too easy to be so driven by the need to advance that the proposed direction can be obscured, making the end goal less attainable. Momentum, particularly at speed, can easily throw missions off course.

Thankfully, a pause for reflection can provide a vital opportunity to reboot. You should regularly take time to review the initial brief and compare the original plan with the current situation.

All objectives improve through objectivity.

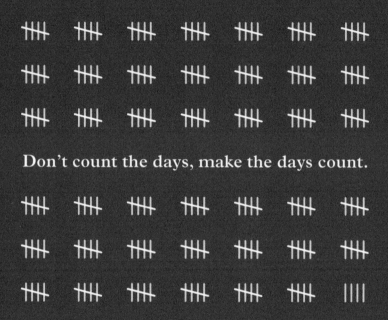

Don't count the days, make the days count.

"

MUHAMMAD ALI

Lived with dyslexia o·······• "Greatest sports personality of the 20th century"

ON
USING
TIME WISELY

Although leaders are inevitably accountable for the successful delivery of an enterprise, they also feel they must carry the burden of every contributing aspect. This is clearly counterproductive and an indicator of poor delegation skills.

It is commonly held that 80% of what you do creates 20% of the impact. Leaders need to reverse this and focus on the 20% of what they do that can make 80% of the impact. You should centre on three or four areas where you can make the most significant contribution.

A leader's own to-do list should be a lot shorter than you probably imagined.

We all have a role
to play in creating
safe environments
where people can
work without fear.

"

ANNA WINTOUR

Fired as junior Fashion Editor after 9 months ○·······● Editor-In-Chief of "Vogue"
for over 30 years

ON
SAFE SPACES

The reason that the world's worst dictatorships have all failed is that they relied on fear to maintain control. History has proved this to be untenable. Fear begets more fear.

Good leadership creates space where the skills of a team can flourish. The mission is communicated clearly, and everyone feels they can express views or make mistakes without aggressive or unconstructive criticism.

In this atmosphere of good faith, should someone fall short, the collective reaction should inevitably be to help. Leaders should positively endorse these behaviours by encouragement and by example.

Productive teams are bound by an unerring sense of trust.

The things which are most important don't always scream the loudest.

"

BOB HAWKE

World record holder for "downing a yard of ale" ○·······● Australian Prime Minister

26

ON URGENT VS IMPORTANT

In any set of circumstances, there can be an unexpected turn of events that will require your immediate attention – inevitably you must execute a response as a reaction.

Mostly though, what is deemed urgent is caused by faulty planning. For example, a rapidly approaching deadline could always have been avoided or unnecessary interruptions not allowed. Every effort should be made to plan *proactively* to avoid being diverted unnecessarily, despite the pleas.

A leader's role is to focus consistently on the end goal. It may not be so urgent, but it will remain unerringly important.

Always keep your eyes on the prize.

The way you step up your game
is not to worry about the other
guy in any situation, because you
can't control the other guy. You
only have control over yourself.
So it's like running a race. The
energy that it takes to look back
and see where the other guys are
takes energy away from you.

"

OPRAH WINFREY

Teenage runaway ○·······● "America's most powerful woman"

27

ON
YOU
NOT THEM

A leader needs little advice on being competitive – it's how they rose to the top. Almost subconsciously, they have felt driven beyond the farthest limits of their abilities.

Maintaining a competitive edge is invaluable for success, creating an energetic spirit of purpose. But focus should always be on your own organisation's performance and how to adjust and optimise it.

Maintaining and exceeding performance levels are constant goals. To become overly preoccupied with the competition's activities can only distract from your team's single-minded sense of purpose.

Concern yourself only with what your competition does in order to inform what you do better.

There's no such thing as getting rid of nervousness.

"

ITZHAK PERLMAN

Living with polio ○·······● Virtuoso violinist and winner of 16 Grammy Awards

28

ON
PUBLIC
SPEAKING

Often, with leadership comes the expectation of addressing groups of people publicly. This does not necessarily come naturally and the prospect can cause anxiety.

What can be overlooked is that usually the audience wants or needs to hear your message – they are seldom hostile, instead looking for relevant information and guidance.

The best way to deal with any spike of nerves is to plan a less intimidating environment. Rehearse so you are at ease with the material. If you prefer to sit then sit; if you prefer to read notes, do so.

Focus on your content and your delivery will follow.

Hear no evil, speak no evil -
and you'll never be invited to a party.

"

OSCAR WILDE

Originally critiqued as "The poet is Wilde   o·······•   The most popular playwright
but the poetry's tame"   in Late Victorian Britain

29

ON
LIFE
AT THE TOP

Before you were given the responsibility of leadership, you would have been a welcome member of the team, regularly invited to join the others at impromptu meetings - often social. Suddenly, when you move up, those invitations dry up.

It's not personal.

Sometimes the team's desire to talk candidly in a relaxed atmosphere makes your presence inhibiting. The robustness of your team is reliant on the respect they have for your leadership. You'll be flattered to know that they would not want to compromise that any more than you would.

Welcome To Lonely Club – you'll be needing some different social outlets.

There is something about building up a comradeship - that I still believe is the greatest of all feats - and sharing in the dangers with your company of peers.

It's the intense effort, the giving of everything you've got. It's really a very pleasant sensation.

"

SIR EDMUND HILLARY

Wounded in WW2 ○········● Member of the first team to reach the summit of Mount Everest

30

ON
JOINING
THE CLUB

Many will talk of the importance of building networks, but a relentless accumulation of contacts is not always the best use of a leader's resources. However, there is a great benefit in sharing experiences with those who are currently to be found in similar positions elsewhere.

Nobody expects – or would want – any confidentiality breaches but it is reassuring to share views concerning general category information, issues or ills currently prevalent in your field.

This provides an outlet that you might not consider appropriate amongst your own team. Talking to those currently doing what you do, acts as a beneficial pressure valve.

It isn't what
they say
about you,
it's what
they whisper.

"

ERROL FLYNN

Fired from his job as a junior shipping clerk ○·······● 18th greatest hero in
American film history

31

ON
RISING ABOVE
THE CHATTER

Gossip is the enemy of collaboration, as it can significantly unsettle morale.

Idle speculation is time-consuming and will inevitably divert attention from your organisation's objectives.

As the leader, this rumour-mongering will inevitably focus on your decision-making more than anyone else's, covering subjects as diverse as your financial package or wardrobe choice. Sometimes, it results from envy, sometimes boredom but you will remain a target because of your position.

It's usually fairly innocuous, so you should avoid reacting; better that the focus is on you than causing dissension amongst the others. However, if there is genuine malice intended, then address it immediately.

The friendship that can cease has never been real.

"

ST. JEROME

Dissolute swinging student ○········● Theologian, historian, translator of the Bible into Latin

32

ON "FRIENDS"

One of the joys of teamwork can be the close bonds that flourish... where they might even be considered friendships.

These are naturally disrupted when you are elevated to a leadership position with responsibility and oversight; a friend's destiny often riding on your decisions.

Some of your "friends" may not respond positively and, owing to their previous proximity, might attempt to unsettle you and unfairly take advantage of your situation.

If friendship is truly unconditional, they should understand the position in which you now find yourself, providing advice and support instead.

If not, then they were just a rival in waiting.

It feels like my hard work has paid off, but at the same time... I still feel like I'm going to wake up, and everybody's going to see me for the hack I am.

"

VIOLA DAVIS

Grew up in poverty ○········• Winner of the 'Triple Crown Of Acting'

33

ON IMPOSTOR SYNDROME

When you engage in a pursuit about which you are passionate, you are desperate to perform it well. Anything less than perfection can feel like failure. Correspondingly, some high achievers feel they do not deserve their success.

It is easy to pass this off as unnecessary humility but really "impostor syndrome" is a genuine problem all leaders can feel – especially in moments of doubt or confusion.

You should regularly consult your own history because there lies the proof of your abilities.

You assumed leadership because somewhere was the confidence that you were the right candidate for the circumstances. Never doubt that.

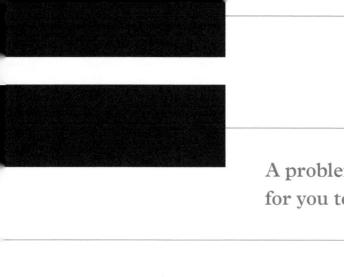

A problem is a chance
for you to do your best.

"

DUKE ELLINGTON

Peanut salesman at   o·······•   Immortal jazz
baseball games   band leader

34

ON
LOVING YOUR
PROBLEMS

It might seem counterintuitive to many, but leaders need to love their problems. However tempting it may be to delay dealing with them, leaders should quickly embrace difficult issues in an effort to take the sting out of any potential repercussions.

Firstly, these problems force swift acceptance of the reality of a situation, and then prompt a change in perspective so that solutions can be found. Leaders should always face up to their environment – however harsh – and take pride in their ability to bring about successful damage limitation.

Without fail, problems will eventually need attention, so always walk towards the gunfire.

Keep your fears to yourself,
but share your courage
with others.

"

ROBERT LOUIS STEVENSON

Burdened with ill health o······• Still the 26th most translated writer in the world

35

ON SHOWING NO FEAR

Fear is terribly contagious. But worse still it multiplies as it descends through an organization. A concern you may air publicly can escalate into something far more corrosive as it takes hold amongst those who may not be in full possession of the facts.

Sometimes, it is best simply to keep your own counsel.

Similarly, your belief and trust in a successful outcome also tends to multiply as it too cascades through an organization. This positive amplification can make your team unstoppable in the pursuit of their objectives.

Fear is toxic... bravery is intoxicating. Make sure to display only the latter.

Don't take criticism from
people you wouldn't normally
go to for advice.

MORGAN FREEMAN

USAF radar repairman ○┄┄┄● Academy Award Winner

36

ON SELECTIVE HEARING

Leaders always attract an unfair share of criticism, and the human tendency is to want to respond to everything. This will only diminish your productivity.

Consider the motivations of your critics. Some will be natural detractors, either through envy of your position or simply their nature, determined to offer unwanted opinions.

If you never deemed these views worth considering beforehand, then, however awkward, ignore them. Time is too valuable.

Conversely, constructive criticism should always be acknowledged. It will be based on knowledge, not conjecture, and so should help shape the path you are forging.

And everyone can only benefit from that.

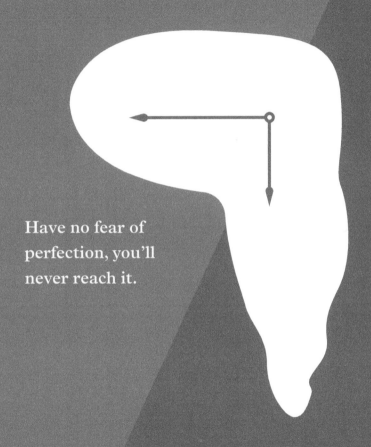

Have no fear of
perfection, you'll
never reach it.

"

SALVADOR DALI

Imprisoned for public disorder ○········● Greatest of all Surrealist artists

37

ON PRECISION OVER PERFECTION

Instinctually, we want everything to be perfect but as the world in which we operate is not, this goal is obviously unachievable. Constant pursuit of perfection can take a heavy toll – a 'mental hamster wheel'.

Leaders are better off substituting perfection, as their objective, with precision.

Focusing on the precision of the team's separate specialisms allows them to demonstrate their subtlety of craft and attention to detail. This approach will instil an all-consuming sense of pride and positive outcomes will follow.

The push for precision in each distinct area ensures that the sum of the parts becomes greater than the whole.

Start where you are.
Use what you have.
Do what you can.

"

ARTHUR ASHE

Sickly child ○········● Three time Grand Slam tennis champion

38

ON EMBRACING CONSTRAINTS

You will always have to deal with constraints – they might constitute shortages of finance, resource or time – but never let them hinder progress. Inactivity is rarely a suitable option.

Instead, use the tools you possess in abundance such as perseverance, collaboration and perhaps, crucially, imagination. The trust put in you as a leader will have emanated from developing numerous coping strategies to work around multiple obstacles towards effective solutions.

Stick to applying the techniques and skills that make up your core strengths and moreover, because you relied on an innovative approach, those results may surprisingly become more positive and more enduring.

To sit back and let fate
play its hand out and
never influence it is
not the way man was
meant to operate.

"

JOHN GLENN

Sold rhubarb to get his first bike ○·······• First American astronaut to orbit
the Earth

39

ON
YOUR
INFLUENCE

Influence is often confused with a shady form of manipulation; but really, it is a legitimate means to break an impasse, allowing you to achieve consensus, re-establish the status quo or simply gain a favourable outcome.

Leadership brings with it the power to influence but it requires a transparent and authentic approach that will avoid recrimination in the future. Maintaining trust lies at the heart of successful influencing.

Consider influence the ability to bring focused attention to a situation – whether a problem or opportunity – that can appeal emotionally or logically to convince others towards the course of action that you recommend.

You will never reach your
destination if you stop and
throw stones at every dog
that barks.

"

WINSTON CHURCHILL

Twice failed entry to Sandhurst   o········●   UK Prime Minister, Nobel Prize
Military Academy   Laureate & one of the 20th Century's
                                                 most significant figures

40

ON GETTING SIDETRACKED

Inevitably, you rose to your position because you have demonstrated an ability to execute a series of tasks successfully and consistently.

But that's no longer your role.

Consequently, others will often plead with you to complete a seemingly straightforward task with which they struggle. You could complete it – and doubtlessly with greater efficiency – but it's their job now. You cannot leave yourself open to becoming mired in unnecessary complications as the project develops – no matter how great the urge to showcase your previous talents.

Advise and educate certainly... but don't get caught up in the weeds.

Otherwise, who's driving the bus?

> For the strength of the wolf is the pack, and the strength of the pack is the wolf. "

RUDYARD KIPLING

Cub reporter ○········• Nobel Prize Laureate

41

ON INTERNAL COMPETITION

Many believe that internal competition is healthy or hugely motivational or even that it reinforces a sense of team spirit.

It doesn't.

It splits your team, creating envy and division. Too much energy and effort are then expended fighting manufactured and unnecessary internal battles, and this will divert from the team's overall objectives.

Effective leaders concern themselves with meshing the team not pulling it apart. They encourage those whose performance needs improvement by using the results of others as a guide for future action, not as a stick to beat them.

The real competition will always be outside your own door.

Never let the fear of striking out,
keep you from playing the game.

"

BABE RUTH

12 years in reform school ○·······• American baseball legend

42

ON
THE PERILS
OF PARALYSIS

A good leader exercises a degree of caution before making key decisions. A pause to reflect is perfectly acceptable but these decisions, however complicated, cannot be left unattended for too long.

Caution can turn into inaction with a heavier significance being placed on any potentially negative consequences. Others can construe this as fear and, fear being contagious, respect for your leadership abilities is rapidly undermined. That's exceptionally hard to win back.

Instead – even if it's to do nothing currently – always frame a decision as a planned move with positive ramifications.

Avoid 'kicking the can' too far down the road.

If you think it's going
to rain, it will.
"

CLINT EASTWOOD

Part-time golf caddy ○·······● Four-time Academy Award Winner

43

ON INVITING TROUBLE

Planning the worst-case scenario is always a key component of drawing up any plan. However, it is unproductive to make that potential outcome your wheelhouse. Being overly pessimistic will inevitably hamper action and therefore progress.

Instead, always keep your thoughts to the upside of the plan foremost in your mind and work towards that. If you have taken due account of the worst case then the element of surprise is gone, and you will know what to do.

However, if you think devils are always at your shoulder, eventually they will take up your subconscious invitation and turn up right there.

Don't walk away from
negative people – RUN!

MARK TWAIN

Left school after 5th grade ○·······● The father of American literature

44

ON DISRUPTIVE ELEMENTS

Teams are inevitably made up of very different personalities – introverts, extroverts, great individual talents, willing workhorses – but they should all understand the objective and therefore their role in achieving it.

Great teams should be able to accommodate this diversity through adept leadership that constantly monitors the respective temperature or fragility of the team's mood.

However, no single individual should be more valuable than the team, no matter what their relationship or specialism. If their actions consistently cause friction, you need to remove them, regardless of reputation and however disruptive to your plans, to safeguard equilibrium.

The team dynamic must come first.

If everyone is thinking alike, then somebody isn't thinking.

GEORGE S. PATTON

Struggled with reading, writing and arithmetic ○········● Highly decorated US General

45

ON ELIMINATING "YES-MEN"

Ultimately, all leaders seek consensus to advance, but that consensus can rarely be achieved without adequate discussion. If your leadership is surrounded by a coterie of "yes-men" then your team is either overcome with fear or a lack of imagination.

Scenario planning needs to investigate the best to worst case outcomes and so the leader should always listen to a spectrum of opinions. Just because they have the mandate to lead, does not mean their initial opinion is always totally correct.

By encouraging the free expression of opinions and views, then the ultimate decision is far more likely to be bulletproof.

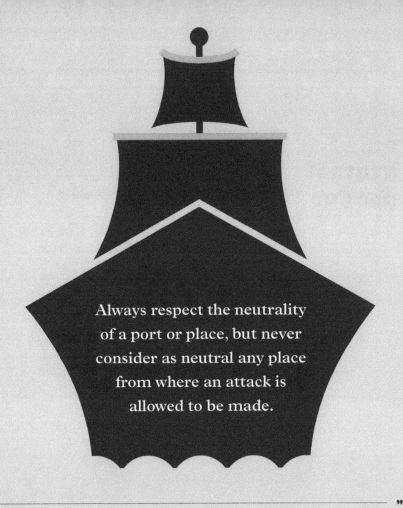

Always respect the neutrality of a port or place, but never consider as neutral any place from where an attack is allowed to be made.

"

HORATIO NELSON

Seasick midshipman ○┈┈┈● British Admiral. Victor of Trafalgar.

46

ON NEUTRAL GROUND

A leader can always face difficult clashes or complaints that demand immediate attention; leaving them to fester would only exacerbate the problem.

Inevitably, this introduces emotional elements – often a sense of bitter grievance.

In this situation, move the discussion to neutral ground, a location associated with neither party. You avoid the unseen (and potentially incendiary) audience, who are eagerly awaiting "the showdown".

A neutral setting immediately calms underlying tensions and allows a more measured discussion and appraisal of the problems. The need to show off is eliminated.

Honestly, some of your most successful executive management will take place in coffee shops.

Few people think more
than two or three times
a year; I have made an
international reputation
for myself by thinking
once or twice a week.

"

GEORGE BERNARD SHAW

Stand-in pianist ○·······● Winner of Nobel Prize for literature and Oscar for
best screenplay

47

ON CLEARING YOUR HEAD

Never underestimate the power of timeout simply to think. You might sit with a coffee, go strolling or even take a bath – whatever suits.

Some time alone just to consider and reflect, could become the best use of time in your entire day.

The problem is inevitably that your headspace is filled with the issues of others and while you are around, they are more than happy to keep adding to them.

Clear the schedule – even for a short time – just to have a few solitary moments. You will be amazed what can emerge even in the smallest gap of downtime.

You can never cross the ocean
until you have the courage to
lose sight of the shore.

"

CHRISTOPHER COLUMBUS

Worked on a cheese stand ○·······● 'Discovered' the New World

48

ON
BRAVE
DECISIONS

All decisions carry elements of uncertainty. However, as a leader, your experience allows you to consider the possible outcomes and make suitable judgements.

Courage requires taking decisions where the ramifications are considerably less clear-cut. Then, you should weigh up this risk versus the possible opportunity – sometimes to thrive and sometimes just to survive.

Inaction can be perceived as weakness by others but a brave yet considered decision will demonstrate command of the situation and instil confidence.

Should that decision prove wrong, circumstances will have changed anyway. A lesson has been learned and experience can guide you to put matters right swiftly.

> Any person capable of angering you becomes your master. "

EPICTETUS

Born into slavery ○·······● Greek Stoic philosopher

49

ON
KEEPING
YOUR COOL

Results do not always go the way you intended; Teams do not always meet the expectations you set; Individuals do not always execute what seems simple to you.

You should always be very careful not to let your frustration boil over into anger. Use this emotion very sparingly.

Screaming and shouting will always make others overly defensive. You lose the necessary ability to be constructive and take control of the team and the situation. You should be finding solutions or imparting lessons in order to avoid any repetition.

The moment you react too forcefully, you lose the opportunity for disciplined dialogue.

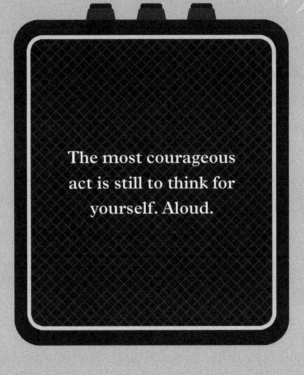

The most courageous act is still to think for yourself. Aloud.

"

COCO CHANEL

Raised in a strict orphanage ○·······● Founder of world-famous fashion house

50

ON
WHAT MAKES
A GOOD
DECISION

Leaders should always try to achieve consensus for mission-critical decisions. Teams should feel involved and consulted as this generates more effective operational dynamics.

However, just because the majority of the group agrees with a proposal, it doesn't necessarily mean it's the right one and if you strongly disagree with the pervading view then do not just quietly acquiesce. Make your case again and be clear about your opposition. Enough will shift because they feel the strength of your conviction.

When leading, the accountability rests with you; so, a majority decision is not a good decision if you don't agree with it.

It is amazing what you can accomplish if you do not care who gets the credit.

HARRY TRUMAN

Worked in newspaper mail room ○·······● 33rd US President

51

ON
OWNING IDEAS

Leaders are most often where they are because they possess a raft of good ideas. But ideas cannot exist in a vacuum, they need their team's buy-in for successful implementation.

Therefore, leaders need to relinquish their sense of individual ownership and let these ideas take root so deeply in others that they adopt them as their own. Further builds may even let them think it was theirs in the first place.

Be happy when this happens. You don't need to put your name on an idea because others' ownership is a signal of their respect for the inclusive process you fostered.

No problem is so deep that it cannot be overcome, given the will of all parties, through discussion and negotiation rather than force and violence.

NELSON MANDELA

Expelled from university ○·······● Madiba – Father of the Nation

52

ON
A GOOD
NEGOTIATION

Mistakenly, the negotiation process can be viewed as entirely competitive with the overall intention of trying to gain the maximum possible for oneself, whilst relinquishing the least to the other side. This adversarial standpoint will create winners and losers... and, more worryingly, long-standing resentments that undermine effective cooperation and destroy loyalty.

Instead, negotiations should be seen as an opportunity to put any relationship onto a mutually beneficial platform with a clear understanding of each party's objectives and expectations.

Enter any negotiation in a positive frame of mind with the intention of resetting the relationship onto a more enduring and secure footing.

Have patience.
All things are difficult
before they become
easy.

"

SAADI

Prisoner of war during The Crusades ○·······● "The Master of Speech"

53

ON
HOLDING
YOUR
HORSES

Sometimes, the elements of a mission take longer to emerge than you might expect. Patience is, naturally, the correct course because impulsive behaviour can derail a plan dramatically.

A show of exasperation will not speed up the process, but it will diminish the confidence of those around you. You just have to let matters play out rather than make a dramatic intervention that can exacerbate the problem further down the line.

Demonstrate outward calmness although inside you may be cursing the delay. If your planning was sound, the results will come.

Patience is not simply waiting... but the art of waiting.

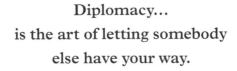

Diplomacy…
is the art of letting somebody
else have your way.

"

SIR DAVID FROST

Gave up training ○·······● Global interviewer & Emmy Lifetime Award winner

54

ON THE DIPLOMATIC ROUTE

Confrontation inevitably drains the levels of both physical and emotional strength so, when possible, it should be avoided. Diplomacy is usually a far more beneficial route to solving problems.

It is emphatically not the art of shuttling between disparate parties but a more subtle skill of working out what exchange may be required to bring someone over to an opinion they had previously opposed.

A strong leader understands the broader motivations behind an opposing argument and looks subsequently to find leverage to break the deadlock more persuasively. Ultimately, you should always be looking to create the right conditions to align objectives.

Talk low, talk slow
and don't talk
too much.

"

JOHN WAYNE

Rejected from the US Naval Academy ○┄┄┄● American movie icon

55

ON
NO FURTHER
COMMENT

Particularly in times of crisis, questions can be fired at a leader repeatedly. If you have a clear response – sometimes only a binary yes or no – then say it and add no more. Often because of the remorseless repetition around the same topic, it is easy to feel compelled to explain further.

The less you say, the less the opportunity to be misrepresented.

If your position remains unchanged, refer to your previous answer. The temptation is to expand but it is potentially damaging. Your position has been made perfectly clear once, that's enough.

If you're in a hole, don't start digging.

Our life is frittered away with detail…
simplify, simplify.

"

HENRY DAVID THOREAU

Worked in a pencil factory ○┄┄┄● Eminent philosopher and natural historian

56

ON SOUNDBITES

Leaders have a responsibility to communicate regularly and communicate clearly. Yet they are usually besieged by information and opinions that are technical and overly detailed. They need to develop the ability to synthesise so that they can subsequently forward any conclusion in a format everybody can understand.

There is a benefit to communication which utilises soundbites or headlines – breaking down the more complex overall message into easily digestible parts. It signposts the key points by transforming the decision into something more memorable and, therefore, actionable.

Soundbites, in the right context, present rallying-points around which teams can easily coalesce and stay focused.

Politics is the art of looking for trouble, finding it everywhere, diagnosing it incorrectly and applying the wrong remedies.

"

GROUCHO MARX

Left school aged 12　○·······●　One of the greatest ever comedians

57

ON SWERVING POLITICS

A politician is supposed to be a person who, through their influence and will, can shape policies to achieve objectives. All leaders obviously need this ability.

However, "being political" now seems to have soured in its meaning. It implies the manipulation of agendas whilst pursuing individual and nefarious goals. Such "politics" can only be damaging to any proposed direction.

The most grievous pitfalls of "political" behaviours manifest themselves as accusations of partiality or prejudice.

True leaders should constantly investigate what motivates a request or proposal and react only to what is beneficial for the mission alone, never for a separate agenda.

It takes
two flints to
make a fire.

LOUISA MAY ALCOTT

Forced to leave school through poverty ○········● Famous American novelist

58

ON
BETTER
TOGETHER

Some believe that the responsibility of leadership requires that all input into the decision-making process should come solely from the leaders themselves. Experience proves that a collaboration is infinitely more beneficial through giving others the opportunity to exhibit their own expertise and judgement.

Teamwork is always a more efficient and productive methodology than autocracy. The leader's role is to ensure the overall vision remains baked into all major discussions and assess contrary opinions, thus maintaining project unity.

Even Darwinian theory supports this; nature is filled with examples of team structures coalescing to allow species to thrive. Humans are really no different.

The whole problem with the world is that fools and fanatics are always so certain of themselves, but wiser people are so full of doubts.

"

BERTRAND RUSSELL

Lonely depressed childhood ○·······● Mathematician, historian, philosopher, writer, social activist etc etc.

59

ON
DARK
MOMENTS

Because leadership can be a lonely business, there will always be moments when leaders doubt themselves and their plans, particularly when carrying the responsibility of asking others to implement their instructions.

These dark periods, compounded by a sense of isolation, can feel personally onerous. But be assured that many great leaders struggled with such moments. Lincoln constantly wrestled emotional demons when faced with difficult decisions; Churchill wrote of the "black dog" at his door.

Don't ascribe any self-blame for having these feelings. This internal questioning is part of the inherent validation and verification process with which all responsible leaders govern themselves.

A desk is a dangerous place from which to view the world.

"

JOHN LE CARRE

Suffered parental abuse o·······• Sold over 60 million books worldwide

60

ON
WALKING
THE FLOOR

Staying put in one place and making all of your team come to you is a particularly unhealthy modus operandi. It advocates a "master and servant" relationship which can be unproductive and appear undemocratic.

By making sure that you associate elsewhere with your team you will get a better understanding of the group dynamics and how they can be improved. Your team will find you more approachable and in turn, you will more likely develop a better early-warning system for any potential problem.

Reducing the barriers between you and your team will help the flow of information and encourage consistent dialogue.

> Appreciation is a wonderful thing:
> it makes what is excellent in others
> belong to us as well.

"

VOLTAIRE

Jailed for insulting the Regent of France ○·······● Leading French writer of
the Enlightenment

61

ON
THANK YOUS

Sometimes, it is easy to forget the effect you can have on your team. Whether consciously or not, they will continue looking to you for affirmation of their performance.

However, because your responsibilities might ordinarily take you away from some of the more routine affairs, your thoughtfulness can also show that you are in touch and remain connected to the entire enterprise.

A word of praise for a job well done counts far more than you might imagine. It shows you have noticed their efforts and, more importantly their role in delivering results.
The benefit to their morale will be immediate.

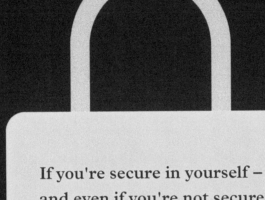

If you're secure in yourself –
and even if you're not secure
in yourself – you don't need
to bully.

"

JOAN JETT

First solo album rejected by 23 major labels   ∘········•   Inducted into the Rock
and Roll Hall Of Fame

62

ON
THE
FUNNY SIDE

Humour is a great icebreaker. It can bond a team together through a shared release and it can relieve the tension in difficult situations.

However, as a leader, you must always be cautious not to look for a cheap laugh at somebody's expense. If there is a barb in what you say – particularly a personal one – remember that it is magnified because it has come from the leader's own mouth. So, the hurt is magnified too. Not everything can just be brushed off as "banter".

Be self-deprecating. Make light of situations. But never forget that jokes are a serious business.

> The sun and moon
> shine on all without partiality.
>
> "

CONFUCIUS

Worked as government book-keeper ○·······● Father of Chinese philosophy

63

ON
HAVING
FAVOURITES

It is virtually impossible not to have favourites – those members of your team that you turn to because you enjoy their company, or you find them unfailingly reliable in delivering your requests. This is permissible whilst you accept the following three provisos.

Firstly, acknowledge your bias, so you can control its perception.

Then, should one of these favourites fail to meet your expectations, do not let it slide without comment.

Finally, never operate this group as a closed shop but instead give everyone the chance to be noticed.

Favouritism is hugely divisive; being a favourite should be an opportunity for all.

Human laziness makes people pigeonhole each other at first sight so that they find nothing in common with each other.

FYODOR DOSTOEVSKY

Incarcerated in a Siberian prison camp ◦········• Major Russian novelist

64

ON
THE
QUIET ONES

They say it takes all sorts to make the world go round but there are many people who feel themselves under-represented through all kinds of stereotyping. Consequently, they find that they are less able to express their view for fear of its dismissal.

Leaders today need to work hard to make sure these views can be expressed safely and without reproach. They need to think about the barriers that might be stifling certain members and if anything – at least early on – overcompensate to allow everyone to feel at ease within the group.

Inclusion does not just require presence but actual participation.

You cannot shake hands
with a clenched fist.

"

INDIRA GANDHI

Lonely awkward teenager ○········● "Iron Lady of India"

65

ON WARRING FACTIONS

Unfortunately, not everybody can get along all the time. The difficulties between opposing factions can devastate a team's equilibrium and, in such a toxic atmosphere, a leader must swiftly extinguish these lingering divisions.

The situation cannot be allowed to drag so an intervention that brings both sides to the table for a frank discussion is imperative. The leader needs to flush out every point causing division, however minor, and then map out a workable solution.

Sometimes, simply airing these grievances can defuse the situation. If not, then a decision is quickly needed about which party should be released from the team.

If you back down from a fear,
the ghost of that fear never goes away.
It diminishes people.

"

HUGH JACKMAN

Part-time PE teacher ○·······● "The Greatest Showman"

66

ON
THREATS

Threats are never an effective negotiating tactic, but, occasionally, they are issued with the intention of pushing a leader into a decision. Threats, no matter how subtle, are a form of bullying and a leader must never be seen to be bullied.

It avoids setting a difficult precedent that others may look to abuse.

The initial fallout may hurt but this is infinitely better than the potential long-term damage to your credibility by not standing firm under pressure.

A leader always remains open to genuine requests but, when issued with provisos, they cease being polite ones. Never bow to any threat.

Confidentiality ███████████████ is ███████

███████████████ the essence ██████████

████████████████████████████████████

███████ of ████████████████████████

████████████ being ████████████ trusted.

"

BILLY GRAHAM

Uncommitted student ○·······● "America's Pastor"

67

ON PRIVILEGED INFORMATION

There are few greater demonstrations of faith than to be taken into someone's confidence. For leaders, these situations will occur frequently. Sometimes, information will be of a personal nature and, sometimes mission-critical.

Confidentiality exists to protect the integrity of the team and the processes they follow, so any breakdown is naturally damaging to the reputation of all parties. This behaviour code should be considered unbreakable.

However, it is sometimes necessary to share your own confidential information and, in so doing, you are always testing the waters of faith and loyalty. Successful leaders know that trust should always be a two-way process.

Life isn't black and white.
It's a million gray areas,
don't you find?

"

RIDLEY SCOTT

Bottom of the class ○·······● Oscar-nominated film director

68

ON
THE HORNS
OF DILEMMAS

"Between a rock and a hard place"; "Damned, if you do, damned, if you don't"; so many of our decisions exist right there. Seldom is it an open and shut case, so leaders need to acclimatise to these less defined areas.

Avoiding decisions is rarely the correct policy, particularly if they lie between two potentially right answers or indeed two least bad ones. Look again at your dilemma by altering the variable factors, and then reconsider each course's respective merits.

If doubt remains, adopt the route that asks more of you, and so can at least support your own internal justification.

Some old-fashioned things like fresh air and sunshine are hard to beat.

LAURA INGALLS WILDER

Never graduated high school ○········● Author of "The Little House On The Prairie" novels

69

ON SLEEPLESS NIGHTS

Leaders are often asked how they sleep when they know they have difficult decisions to make – especially ones with harsh personal consequences. Sometimes, they honestly just don't sleep at all.

After all, these outcomes cannot be taken lightly, and leaders are human too. It is, therefore, their duty to take as much care of themselves as possible. They cannot afford to burn the candle at both ends, because clear heads are always needed.

As you will have to manage the bad news fallout, carve out some private time to recover your own equilibrium. It will be called upon again soon enough.

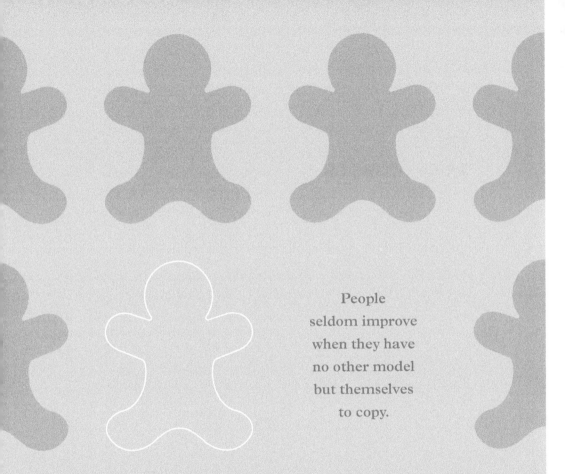

People
seldom improve
when they have
no other model
but themselves
to copy.

"

OLIVER GOLDSMITH

Expelled from university for rioting ○········● Renowned playwright and poet

70

ON
ROLE MODELS

Before assuming any leadership position, you will have inevitably encountered leaders who have served to inspire your own development. There might also be other figures whose characteristics you admire – perhaps from history or your outside interests.

Sometimes, there's an impasse in your decision-making where solutions stubbornly refuse to emerge. A useful starting point is to take your inspirational source and consider what they would do in similar circumstances. Don't slavishly adhere to their methodology – you're not a facsimile after all – but this can provide a creative launchpad either to build on or react against.

So, ask yourself, "what would they do?"

The source of everything
respectable in man... is that
his errors are CORRIGIBLE.

"

JOHN STUART MILL

Teenage depressive ○·······● "The most influential English speaking
philosopher of the 19th century"

71

ON
GIVING
CRITICISM

It seems obvious that leaders should point out errors to their team when they make them. But often, they fail to do so. Sometimes, it is borne out of a fear of confrontation or desire not to diminish one's popularity.

But this is weakness.

Avoid unnecessary aggression, of course – even if confronted adversely – but criticism represents a clear demonstration of a commitment to the individual's development. Prepare to be candid but always constructive.

You have as great an obligation to provide criticism as you do to pass on positive feedback, and it will consequently enhance respect for your position.

The characteristic shared by people at the top of their profession is that, to get better, they crave criticism.

"

SEBASTIAN COE

Asthmatic ○·······● Broke 3 athletics world records in 41 days

72

ON
TAKING
CRITICISM

Leaders, by their very nature, find themselves in exposed positions and so easy targets for criticism – not all of it necessarily constructive. We are only human so it can hurt.

However, you should never react violently or impulsively as inevitably, this will compound the gravity of the situation and leave you open to further criticism.

Instead use it as a spur for improvement because, after all, however painful, there may be an element of truth. Think of all criticism as a personal temperature check – an indication (like a fever) that something may need investigation. Your diagnosis will be what matters most.

It's always
better to leave
the party early.

"

BILL WATTERSON

Fired from "The Cincinnati Post" ○·······● Creator of "Calvin & Hobbes"

73

ON
GOING OUT

Successful teams often socialise together. It allows people to get to know each other better in a relaxed environment and the informality draws out a team's commonalities.

These gatherings can show a leader's more human side normally unseen within the team context.

They want to perceive a leader as interesting, good company and subsequently more approachable.

However, the leader has nothing to prove in social settings. Be careful not to end up in a situation that can diminish your position of respect. However informal, all eyes remain on you.

In short: Don't be the last one standing at the bar.

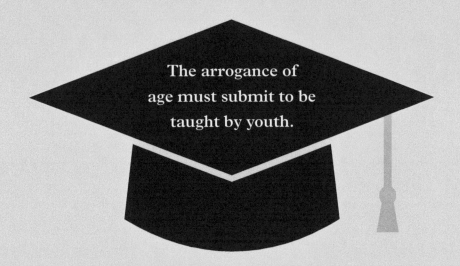

The arrogance of age must submit to be taught by youth.

"

EDMUND BURKE

Dropped out of studies to go "wandering" ○·······• Founder of modern Conservatism

74

ON
"YOUNG FOLK"

It is valuable for leaders to take counsel from outside their core team, particularly from their younger recruits.

Inevitably they are more in touch with present realities and more deeply concerned with future prospects. Their viewpoint can act as a barometer of current situations, and even as an early warning for potential bumps in the road.

Paying attention to them, when others might choose to overlook them, will also make them feel more closely tied to the enterprise.

Engaging with your younger talents will always bring a fresh and beneficial perspective on the world outside the one where you normally operate.

I, in recognizing the frailties and the requirements of human nature, would rather try to persuade a man to go along, because once I have persuaded him, he will stick. If I scare him, he will stay just as long as he is scared, and then he is gone.

"

DWIGHT D. EISENHOWER

Night supervisor   ∘·······•   Supreme Allied Commander & 34th US President

75

ON BUILDING LOYALTY

They say that you should try to lead by example. This generates respect amongst your team and respect builds loyalty. Loyalty is the undisputed unifier of any successful team.

Leadership requires empathy – the ability to understand another's situation whilst offering the opportunity to help. A team will perform more productively if they are persuaded rather than berated.

If they are not brought around but simply act out of fear, they will never commit properly to the overall objective.

However, a more persuasive attitude allows you to allay concerns and dispel uncertainty. Consequently, the atmosphere is one of single-mindedness towards the goal.

First-rate people
hire first-rate people;
second-rate people
hire third-rate people.

"

LEO ROSTEN

Polish refugee   o·······•   Acclaimed humorist and Hollywood screenwriter

76

ON
HIRING

Never be the smartest person in the room.

A good leader engages people much smarter than themself. You need people with superior and specialized talents and then just allow them to get on and use them. They require little management consequently, and you can point yourself elsewhere.

Naturally, you might want to appear the best at everything, believing (wrongly) you are leading by example. But the opposite is true; your team will feel handicapped.

Create space for these talents to flourish and you'll achieve stronger results.

Don't feel threatened – weren't you the one who made that excellent recruitment decision after all?

A lot of different flowers make a bouquet.

ISLAMIC PROVERB

77

ON
A RANGE
OF OPINIONS

Paying lip service to diversity and inclusion for the sake of political correctness or a box ticking exercise should never be considered permissible. These are not just forms of organizational hygiene, because the future of any enterprise will entirely depend on a leader's genuine support of them.

Great decisions always demand diagnosis and that requires stress-testing ideas. This is best achieved when a broad selection of different interpretations and advocates are actively encouraged to contribute to the review. Creating cookie-cutter cliques of uniformity stifles expression and limits opportunity.

To open our minds, we must also resolutely open our eyes and our ears.

The only reason people do not know
much is because they do not care to know.
They are incurious. Incuriosity is the
oddest and most foolish failing there is.

"

STEPHEN FRY

Struggles with bipolar disorder ○·······● Prolific writer, broadcaster, performer
and national treasure

78

ON
DELVING
DEEPER

One of the most enjoyable aspects of leadership is that you gain an oversight of areas and specialisms to which you will have had less exposure previously. Nobody expects you to be an expert but if you're the ultimate decision maker then it is always beneficial to explore more widely.

Your team will inevitably appreciate you spending time to understand better their role in the overall scheme and how, from your new perspective, you might help them. Furthermore, you obtain a sense of how the enterprise joins up and so can perform more effectively.

Let every day become a school day.

The leaders who offer blood, toil, tears and sweat always get more out of their followers than those who offer safety and a good time. When it comes to the pinch, human beings are heroic. "

GEORGE ORWELL

Colonial policeman ○·······● Author of "1984" and "Animal Farm"

79

ON
SETTING
CHALLENGES

Challenges are not supposed to be easy. but they represent an opportunity to complete something that has not previously been achieved under your leadership.

When you lead the briefing, there is no point in soft-soaping the energy levels required. If you have brought the right people onto the team, they will be enthused at the prospect of taking on new objectives. A team left simply to manage the status quo can easily become distracted elsewhere and instead seek another outlet for their energies. That's potentially damaging to any enterprise.

Constantly setting new challenges will keep the team spirit focused and fresh.

The most important thing in a leader is ownership. Leaders must not be afraid of owning up to mistakes, things that are not great, and should not be afraid of standing up to them.

"

SERENA WILLIAMS

Diagnosed with Sjögren's syndrome   ○········•   More tennis Grand Slam titles in the open era than any other female player

80

ON
MEA CULPA

Humility is a welcome trait in leaders and an admission that they themselves have made an error, is important in showing their humanity. Admission is never a sign of weakness but of strength.

Choosing not to admit to an error serves only to confirm the likelihood of repeating it and this will erode confidence. The best way to reaffirm your ability in the eyes of your team, is to correct the problem and move forward.

Whilst your pride may be dented, fallibility is forgivable when harnessed to honesty. The real error is always in not owning up to making the mistake.

> Bad news isn't wine. It doesn't improve with age. "

COLIN POWELL

Worked in a furniture store ○········● First African-American Secretary of State

81

ON
BAD NEWS

Delivering bad news is never easy because the reaction to it is often emotionally charged or unpredictable. Therefore, the temptation is to lighten the news by minimizing it or framing it with more positive additions.

Neither is a good ploy; the recipient is likely to miss the significance of the news, believing it not so serious or focusing on the positive instead.

Leaders need to be direct, however painful, but then immediately demonstrate the assistance they can give in coping with any potentially turbulent consequences. Your clarity and support will provide a reassurance that will prove particularly valuable at that time.

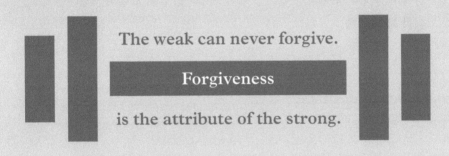

The weak can never forgive.

Forgiveness

is the attribute of the strong.

MAHATMA GANDHI

Average student ○········● Founding father of Indian independence

82

ON
FORGIVING
ERRORS

Anyone – literally anyone – can make a mistake. They are rarely deliberate but elicit huge anxiety to those who caused them. Leaders have two duties; firstly, and most obviously to advise on fixing the resulting problem.

Then, they should investigate why the mistake occurred; Perhaps a lack of understanding? Poor judgement? Personal issues?

Regardless, forgiveness should always be the default response. Don't think of the transgression as a cause of blame but an opportunity to learn.

However, if the lessons remain unlearned and the same mistakes repeated then it won't be coincidence... just a pattern of behaviour you couldn't spot until then.

The time is always

right

to do what is

right

"

MARTIN LUTHER KING

Dreamed of being a fireman   ○········●   Leader of the Civil Rights Movement

83

ON
MORAL
IMPERATIVES

Regardless of status, everyone can be held accountable for their actions. However, because leaders set the tone for others to follow, the responsibility to act with integrity is even higher.

They should always be clearly guided by their moral compass pointing them towards doing the right thing, regardless of any potential personal gain.

However, this behaviour code cannot just be for public display, but in private too.

If you are looking at yourself in the mirror and think you are not doing the right thing... then you are *not* doing the right thing. Correct it immediately, however hard that may be.

A problem shared is
a problem halved.

PROVERB

84

ON SHOWING COMPASSION

People will come to you with problems because they genuinely need your help.

To make them feel more comfortable, the natural tendency is to mirror their experience with your own, hoping they will feel less troubled because you went through the same.

This, unfortunately, replaces their seemingly relieved burden by subconsciously taking on yours. They may not come again, believing that they are already adding to your own pile of problems.

Instead, show sensitivity by just listening – because unburdening is cathartic – and use any shared experience simply to provide possible solutions.

This is, after all, why they came to you originally.

We're here for a reason.
I believe a bit of the
reason is to throw
little torches out
to lead people
through the
dark.

"

WHOOPI GOLDBERG

Mortuary attendant ○·······● Winner of an Emmy, Grammy, Tony & Oscar

85

ON
BEING
A MENTOR

There is no point having a team without seeking to develop and improve it. Training is essential for every success but, because teams need to be made up of different characters, mentoring needs to identify as a dialogue not a series of instructions.

Your effect on the team is immense but do not fall into the trap of creating 'mini-replicas' of yourself. Mentoring should encourage personalities and ultimately allow them to shine on their own merits.

Listen, advise, support – you'll see the rewards take shape as a result, whilst reaffirming your own sense of value because of the role you played.

If I have seen further,
it is by standing on the
shoulders of giants.

"

ISAAC NEWTON

Failed farmer ○·······● Founder of the principles of Modern Physics

86

ON BEING MENTORED

Whilst the role of a leader is to offer mentorship to those they want to grow, it does not mean that they themselves no longer require something similar. One could even propose the need is even greater.

The acceptance of a mentor acting as a leader's sounding board has been a proven success throughout history – think Aristotle to Alexander the Great.

Through their previous experience, a mentor can provide perspective on many issues, especially in unfamiliar situations. The opportunity to talk through options from another viewpoint will improve your own clarity and more robust solutions will surely emerge.

Iron sharpens iron.

Education
is not the filling
of a pail, but the
lighting of a fire.

"

WILLIAM BUTLER YEATS

Underwhelming student, poor at spelling ○······● Nobel Prize Winner for
Literature

87

ON
STAYING
CURIOUS

Whilst leaders aim to accomplish their objectives with perfect execution, their true colours emerge through their ability to adapt to changing situations. When one objective is achieved, another one quickly presents itself. They create a knowledge base of potential solutions, borne out of their experience and desire to keep learning.

Hence, your leadership will develop continually as an iterative process. There is no limit to what could be useful in your armoury so maintain an open mind soaking up as much information as possible.

There is no predicting what you may find, nor when you could put it to good use.

The art of life is a
constant readjustment
to our surroundings.

"

OKAKURA KAKUZO

Dismissed from the Tokyo   ○·······●   Authored "The Book Of Tea" and responsible
School of Arts   for opening Japanese art to the West

88

ON
TEAM
CHANGES

Occasionally, the composition of an organization or team will need to change – sometimes involuntarily and sometimes because it requires a fresh outlook. This change can cause uncertainty with other members and their circle, citing all manner of potential disruptions as a result of this upheaval.

Hold your nerve. The key is to have a plan in place for the new situation and communicate that at the same time, leaving no hiatus in the flow of information, whenever possible.

It is unfailingly remarkable that humans have such short memory spans after a replacement plan has been implemented clearly, swiftly and without fuss.

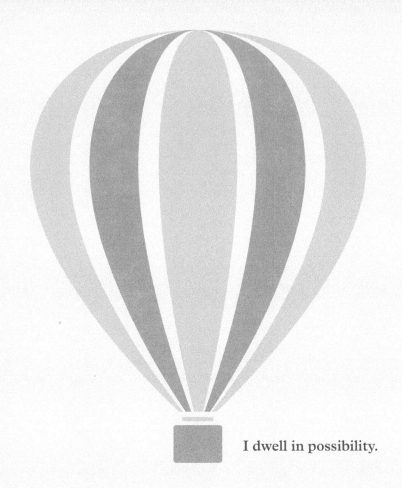

I dwell in possibility.

"

EMILY DICKINSON

10 poems published in her lifetime ○·······● Constantly in print since 1890

89

ON STAYING AHEAD

Everywhere, the world is changing faster and faster, so leaders need to think ahead of the curve by keeping an eye on all current developments in their field and opening regular discussion on how to take advantage of these movements proactively.

They should actively encourage their team to think in terms of "can if..." rather than "can't because...". After all, if necessary, any rulebook can be torn up.

They need to stay on top of the intelligence in order to update their thinking regularly. Innovation is not just about invention but the rare ability to unlearn, relearn and master new skills.

It's not about changing people,
sometimes it's about changing a situation.
How can we build an even better situation for them?

"

JURGEN KLOPP

Video rental shop employee ○·······● UEFA Champions League-winning manager

90

ON UNDER- PERFORMERS

Substandard performance can be costly to a team's dynamic. It can diminish the work of the other members and correspondingly, provoke dissension.

The temptation is to remove the underperformer immediately. However, replacement can be equally costly in terms of time, resource and effort, for acclimatizing new members.

Your inclination instead should be to examine the underlying reasons and look to alleviate them purposefully.

It might require some retraining, prescribing rest or a simple discussion clarifying expectations. But, by first asking how to help, you will give yourself the best chance of restoring equilibrium quickly.

Understanding is a cornerstone of successful leadership.

You have to leave the city of your comfort and go into the wilderness of your intuition. What you'll discover will be wonderful. What you'll discover is yourself.

ALAN ALDA

Polio sufferer ○·······● 5-time Emmy Winner

91

ON
CHECKING IN

Being judged by ultimate outcomes cannot be the only criteria leaders use so they should be prepared to assess themselves on a regular basis.

To lead effectively, they need to be able to flex to the constantly changing conditions and attitudes of their team's dynamic and mission. In order to keep on top of this, they should constantly look at how they are able to adapt and what needs to be adjusted within their own management style. It may create a feeling of vulnerability but also of actionable honesty.

Good leadership is an ongoing process and needs regular and authentic self-appraisal.

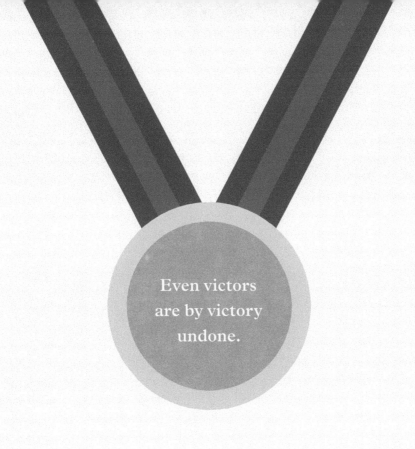

Even victors
are by victory
undone.

"

JOHN DRYDEN

Thrown out of The Royal Society ○·······● England's 1st Poet Laureate

92

ON HUMILITY IN VICTORY

Kipling talked of triumph and disaster as "twin impostors" and the margin between the two is often very narrow. He advises acting with equanimity to both.

There are few things better for morale than success, and leaders should allow their team to enjoy such moments. However, it is also very important for them to avoid over-celebrating. After all, next time may have a different outcome and a measured approach would be equally welcome.

Lacking humility in moments of triumph can often imply that they are rare occurrences, thereby sending out signals that can sow seeds of doubt concerning their leadership abilities.

> In victory,
> you deserve
> champagne.
> In defeat,
> you need it. "

NAPOLEON BONAPARTE

Bullied at school ○·······• French Emperor & brilliant military strategist

93

ON POST-MORTEMS

The ever-increasing capacity of our collective inboxes means that we unwittingly ignore the opportunity to reflect on a project's outcome. Often, we find ourselves too consumed by our next activity.

However, good leaders will always take the opportunity to review performance with their team – whether the outcome was positive or negative. This reinforces the importance of teamwork and showcases experiences for subsequent situations.

You should ensure that the review happens, regardless of time pressure. It creates a meaningful forum for group discussion whilst drawing a line under any underlying issues that might linger.

And sometimes, it's just nice to taste victory.

Celebrate what you've accomplished

but raise the bar a little higher,

every time you succeed.

"

MIA HAMM

Born with a club foot ○·······● Twice FIFA World Footballer of the Year

94

ON
RESETTING

Leaders should always view failure through a positive lens – the opportunity to learn and carry out the task better next time. These often provide watershed moments.

Success should be viewed similarly.

Attaining a goal should rightly be celebrated as it acknowledges all efforts made to achieve a job well done. However, it should also serve as a nudge to set higher standards of what could potentially be achieved. Teams are motivated by challenges and are likely to remain loyal to the cause, while you provide opportunities, others elsewhere cannot. Human nature relishes such chances to be inspired.

Always ask, "What's next?".

For fast-acting relief,
try slowing down.

"

LILY TOMLIN

Waitress at Howard Johnsons ∘·······• Winner of Grammy, Emmy and
Tony Awards

95

ON
TAKING
TIME OFF

Everybody considers themselves to be indispensable, leaders often even more so. They fear that without their presence the overall objective may somehow become derailed.

This is very unlikely. The right team and the right briefing should allow you to take a much-needed break. You need to trust them.

Downtime is crucial for the maintenance of your mental and physical equilibrium and correspondingly, your powers of judgement. Decision-making is an exhausting process, and a tired mind will not always see the subtleties of situations. Rest brings renewal.

So, book that vacation because even the prospect of it will serve to inspire you.

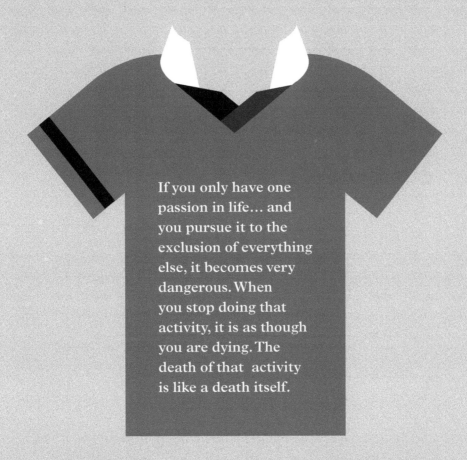

If you only have one passion in life… and you pursue it to the exclusion of everything else, it becomes very dangerous. When you stop doing that activity, it is as though you are dying. The death of that activity is like a death itself.

"

ERIC CANTONA

Banned 6 times from playing when young   ○·······●   One of FIFA's 100 Greatest living players

96

ON EXTRA-CURRICULARS

Taking charge of a team or project can become all-consuming. This is not a healthy situation because as rounded human beings, we all need interests elsewhere.

It is essential that you make time to pursue other passions. These are what ground us – maybe family, friends, or pastimes. Alternating your focus in a different environment can help maintain your overall levels of concentration.

Your leadership style becomes more compelling by utilising a different, yet personal, set of references to bring the mission to life.

Inspiration can come from all around us, and time spent occupied elsewhere can surprisingly illuminate your leadership challenges.

He who has never learned to obey
cannot be a good commander.

"

ARISTOTLE

Suffered discrimination as a Macedonian   ○········●   Philosopher, teacher and the
in Athens   first recorded scientist

97

ON
FOLLOWING

It may seem paradoxical but good leaders should also, when necessary, be good followers. They are well-placed to understand the exhausting demands of leadership without undermining the integrity of the team.

They will collaborate easily and understand how to implement an instruction. Importantly, they should be able through their experience, to communicate clearly and contribute to debate without dominating the discussion.

Success is derived from a two-way exchange of unflinching commitment to the team's objective, regardless of where in the structure you currently sit.

Great leaders focus on their followers, while great followers focus on making their leaders road less rocky.

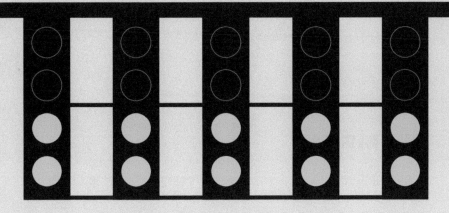

When it's time to go on, it's time to go on and when you get up there you either croak, puke, fall over... or not.

"

KEITH RICHARDS

Expelled from school o·······• Creator of "Rock's single greatest body of riffs"

98

ON
THE BIG DAY

Every team has a set-piece moment that they work towards – a meeting, a performance, an event or even a match – and it can dominate everyone's focus... sometimes to the point where it can inject a debilitating fear of failure.

Leaders, especially, feel the pressure as they carry everyone's expectations with them. Stay calm and remind your team that this is the culmination of all their preparations. Everyone knows their role, from build-up to conclusion, including contingencies. You trust them; they trust you; you all know you can succeed. Work to your plan not the occasion.

What's the worst that can happen?

A society grows great when old men
plant trees whose shade they know
they will never sit in.

"

GREEK PROVERB

99

ON
SUCCESSION

Even though it may be early in the tenure of your leadership, it is important to identify people with the potential to be your successor. Your opinion may change later but begin to expose any possible candidates to some – though inevitably not all – of the intricacies of leadership.

This is not official training but will ensure that they will not come upon some of the issues entirely cold. Furthermore, it allows others to feel confident that the mission can be maintained without hiatus or uncertainty.

A smooth transition to your successor is one of the most important legacies you can leave.

Always quit for the day, when you know what you want to do next.

ERNEST HEMINGWAY

Junior reporter ○········● Winner of Nobel Prize for Literature

100

ON
WHEN
TO MOVE ON

Almost from the start, there will be speculation about how long you should be in your leadership position. Indeed, you will probably be regularly conducting your own personal introspection on the subject.

Other openings can be enticing, but they involve starting over and stepping into the unknown. The first rule is to consider whether there is enough opportunity to merit changing environment.

However, the other factor to consider is whether you still have opportunity within your current role. Only if the role has become tedious through repetition, have you probably run out of track.

Opportunity should always trump any other inducement.

To get through the hardest journey we need take only one step at a time, but we must keep on stepping.

"

CHINESE PROVERB

101

ON
YOUR
JOURNEY

Leadership is a journey... and often not an easy one. You will make mistakes and take wrong turns, but as long as you learn, then any effort was surely worthwhile. You will gain wider knowledge, yet crave wider still.

Ultimately, you are the shaper of success and not just your own. With it, comes the responsibility of carrying the hopes of others and this can also serve as a source of great pride and, quite possibly, admiration. Your energy will ignite their fire.

Let your antenna buzz. Let your synapses snap.

Leadership will change you... for the better.

Best get started.

CPSIA information can be obtained
at www.ICGtesting.com
Printed in the USA
LVHW072239240522
719535LV00019B/660